SPIRAL TRACE

OTHER BOOKS BY JACK MARSHALL

The Steel Veil

From Baghdad to Brooklyn

Gorgeous Chaos

Millennium Fever

Chaos Comics

Sesame

Arabian Nights

Arriving on the Playing Fields of Paradise

Bits of Thirst

Surviving in America

Floats

Bearings

The Darkest Continent

Spiral
Trace

A Poem by Jack Marshall

COFFEE HOUSE PRESS

Minneapolis

2013

Coffee House Press books are available to the trade through our primary distributor, Consortium Book Sales & Distribution, cbsd.com. For personal orders, catalogs, or other information, write to: Coffee House Press, 79 Thirteenth Avenue NE, Suite 110, Minneapolis, MN 55413.

Coffee House Press is a nonprofit literary publishing house. Support from private foundations, corporate giving programs, government programs, and generous individuals helps make the publication of our books possible. We gratefully acknowledge their support in detail in the back of this book.

Good books are brewing at coffeehousepress.org

LIBRARY OF CONGRESS CATALOGING-IN-PUBLICATION DATA

Marshall, Jack, 1936–

Spiral trace : a poem / by Jack Marshall.

p. cm.

ISBN 978-1-56689-327-5 (alk. paper)

I. Title.

PS3563.A722S65 2013

811'.54—DC23

2012036529

PRINTED IN THE UNITED STATES

Some of these poems originally appeared in the following online journals: *Slate*, *Poetry Flash*, *Contemporary World Poetry*, *Emprise Review*, *Perigee*, and *Serving House Journal*.

I wish to thank the Guggenheim Foundation for a grant, which was of great help in writing this book.

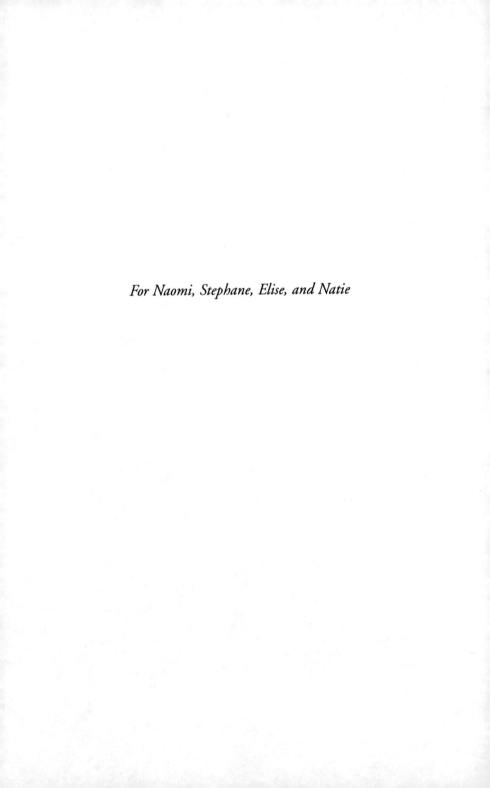

For Naomi, Stephane, Elise, and Natie

The Beautiful Hidden

He was talking about "the hidden." He had
come from chemo. We sat in the car.
Facing straight ahead,

he looked too tired to turn
and face me.
His friend had driven him

and stopped to chat. "His mind is
pure, his house is a mess;
he's a pain in the ass,"

she said. "I take him every week." Rapt,
he faced front in the passenger seat, still
as a mummy just out of the crypt,

with all the time behind him staring at all
that lay ahead. To see
such zeal

was not to envy it.
It wasn't patience, more like practiced
foreboding, which might

foresee the unseeable, which could
not be seen
before it is," he said.

"The beautiful does not exist
somewhere before it is
bidden and made manifest;

it is not waiting to be seen.
It comes from the force of attraction and life-
giving power." . . . Then,

I swear, out of nowhere, two deer
come clattering down the street, two mighty, meaty
four-hooved tap dancers

on tiptoe,
skidding sparks, at the intersection
stop, look off: a deer and a doe in El Cerrito,

peering toward San Pablo Avenue, tails
twitching panic in their pause, turn,
and head toward the hills.

SPIRAL TRACE

1—

Shadows not yet
their darkest, clouds
no longer white,

squabbling birds twitter
on the branch
for turns at the feeder;

dipping white moth wings
above the last blossoms,
dabbing . . .

Light, air,
levitating
vapor;

no procession slow
as clouds turn so stately
taffy . . . There goes

a hefty baguette, lapped after
by goose-necked, omnivorous monkey-
lipped Mick Jagger,

tongue-loop on the rise, as winking
sunset is an eye
dimming, shrinking

to a mote you see go by
that bids your lid
blink, and spy

fading light's
future in fading
sight,

as when the eye
takes in too much
light to see;

like having a cloud for a sty
you try
to see

through sunset's last hour,
silken light on a silo
gathering splendor.

Sometimes it can take all day
to put self-absorption away
before beginning the day . . .

and though I am not choosing
to go where I cannot see,
I am losing.

We are like morphing clouds
who hold our shape
no more than a mood;

now shrill crickets tick
fig-seed clusters thick
in testicular sacs,

now the soft feel
of wrinkled firmness
in the ripe fig's heel.

Here we go the lilac way
the close of day goes
down, a lava flow.

Polluted pink above hills,
granular citron above pink,
darkening blueness above it all

cool
the spark bringing days
to a burnished boil.

2—

This is the silhouette hour; edges,
fractal filigree
on the horizon's ledge;

the sharper the outline,
the dimmer
the horizon.

Then a flash—
sunset-breasted finch across the trellis—
holds you astonished,

as when a window
on what had closed in a life
opens and looking through

oncoming violet light lulls
a lingering stare.
After seventy, the self's fuel,

running out, falls out of love
with itself into a new stammering
grammar of grief,

with less reason
left for self-
satisfaction

as you sense there
is no other side—crossing
over is *being* over.

To see that bearing
down is to see deeper
jungle in the clearing.

No escape, only lulls
in summer warming
cluster-bomb shrapnel.

A mouth that says "the soul"
hasn't said a thing
about the real

news, our need's
fix that famishes
what it feeds:

horror-filled
airtime
bloated with visual

gore, keeping jobs
reporting everyone else
losing theirs to techies in Punjab.

Do movies
affect us differently
than TV news;

how can their images
in the mind
not merge?

I'm not claiming anything which no-
body doesn't
already know.

Do I repeat you?
Then two
of us do.

From Mumbai speaks the other
side of the planet.
There too, no cure

in the great planetary sausage machine.
Wherever there's geography
grief grinds out television.

At a mall's super-sized TV wall, we stop
at an Afghan wedding
smart-bombed while we shop,

bride and groom in mangled embrace,
cut to twenty sets flashing
candy-colored toothpaste.

3—

Hello, hello, I am returning
the human phone call
concerning being

here, in a continuum
passing in the near-
silent hum.

Great! In sunlight,
writing about
sunlight! How great

a periwinkle's petals
shrink-wrap the blue
sky at eye level.

Then nearly dozing, comes
a moment that steadies
space on a stem.

Sky's light from the inner core,
in the blinding kiln,
reflects a silicone mirror,

as if the sun's heat
turns your insides
out.

Only on the way
down does the sun
make my day,

as in a grove of trees, a stroll
will smell of pharmacy
eucalyptus, sage, menthol.

Though some hope of delight has
to make a crack in the darkness,
and sometimes does,

when the sun goes
and darkness grows, you want more
than what the day shows;

more than what grows dim
with age, and we steadily
fade from;

each day's necessity
calling for what's no longer
possible for tomorrow's emergency.

Long day, light's great swill
now approaches an hour
when all colors are still,

and sunset's ghost eyes
glint
from opposite windows.

From the claret-
edged horizon-rimmed
goblet,

drink the blue infinite
cooling
creation's heat,

and the eye
that holds you,
lets go.

4—

Here's a narrative you
won't find
in the news:

In my weekly call to Renee, I tell her
lobsters in Maine used to
cost a dollar; she answers,

"Mr. Used To
died a long time ago."
That was ten years ago.

The dead we remember as beams
of light come into our life
gathered in a lens. We are that lens.

In mom's and Aunt Becky's eyes,
Renee said near the end,
a look told her, in ways

without word or signal,
"On the stairway of days
you climb, there is no handrail,

unlike us who have no need
of hand, rail, or days,
and when you call, pay you no heed."

I heed; they accelerate—
faces sucked into the sky—
speck, smudge, mote—

and with them,
the world of sight and sound
crossing gravity's barrier in

a blur over the horizon
arc, sinking in,
erasing all outline

but what sundown
makes silhouettes
of cut-out tin,

and a light not only for eyes
appears and weighs
on us.

Is there a presence,
in trees, shadows, living creatures,
of those absent? Absence—

our second world? With eyes
barely brushed
by what's left to see

of those who are gone? They seem
never to have been real,
but, as we will be, dreamed.

5—

Bent barbed bloom
beside the archway:
black sunflower in ruin . . .

I'm tickled it's called
"black" for its deeply purple
seeds and petals. Could well

be title for this poem:
"Black Sunflower," words so
at odds delight when

they bind and interweave
and make sunlight visible
laughter from leaf to leaf,

and the mini-trampolines between tree
limbs, silver-threaded
pulsing mandalas on a breeze.

Does that make art
therapy? Maybe;
maybe not.

But can imagining a fuller life
than you
actually live

make you sigh,
and feel better
about going to die?

Eventual loss,
flowing back to
present choices

we make, is what made
Hart Crane, so alive
to opposites unreconciled

in himself, retire in
the sea and survive
all coffins.

Dour, drunken William Faulkner had
no other way
to caress the world

than his furious,
breakneck time-
stopping prose.

And Rothko: "To steal
for yourself a place
on the rich man's wall,"

and make a place
out of forms that will not stay
in place:

radiance about to go wild,
serenity
about to explode.

Pollock was never splashier
than when hitting the tree. Art,
upping the ante, is not more

than wishful thinking made
for running the whole way
on your hands at incredible speed,

and melodies that vanish
before they've been
caught as wishes.

As earthworms seeking a mate
overcome for a time
their dread of light,

what's called forth holds
more shocks, too
fast to see motion's goal,

which you can't see
until you've said
what speaking will free,

that everything spoken
stems from the not yet, the
not spoken

speech
which points
to no speech,

and the unmeaning of the said,
and the meaning of the unsaid,
lead

at last to a taste
for less
than least.

6—

"In the Great Depression, people told
the same story over and over:
that's all they had

to share." Out of the boat-hold,
he saw the streets of New York
not paved with gold,

but with unemployed; in summer heat
on the Dakota plains, the endless gold
of the fields was not gold, but wheat.

And now depression is
clinically redefined
as "mere sadness"? . . .

as if not deserving
to bear the weight
put on by living;

nothing Zoloft can't cure
down to the normal
medical sure

thing. Regard the murderer as he
regards himself: the victim
he used to be.

The young man on Death Row
for killing his parents: "I did it
in revenge for being alive." Wow!—

That's it: avenge, or live,
and forgive
being alive!

War
is making Iraqi children
smaller.

In Baghdad, kids videoed at home
sobbing over parents gunned down
before their eyes, wilder than

is bearable; faces
wrenched with the horror
in their voices.

Are faces of American children
forced to such
contortions

on a daily basis?
Makes for
a different kind of face:

fear like a hot river races
through; terror stays, terror
transfixes.

If our children do—and they may—,
it will go hard
with us one day.

That hot mama via in vitro fertilizer
must be laying up a store
of survivors for the future.

So, rise and hurry as you will,
you'll see your children
against a wall, yourself as well.

Trying to write
faster than my eyes
are losing sight—

grayer,
hazier,
ghostlier—

and already beginning
to give thanks,
as though going

blind would be a union
of sorts with such
a sun.

I like sunlight most
when my eyes
are closed,

or when a movement—small
enough, and surrounded by
stillness—startles.

7—

In the rushing waters
of always
one thing more, here

come hummers en masse for honey
and pollen they suck
like seed money;

who must sip twice their weight
each day to stay
in flight,

as September stretches
thin between rising
costs and stagnant wages

at war with the gangrene
of government given to
market-driven mysticism.

Weighed down
by the money belt
that did him in,

Rimbaud in Africa
hoped to learn,
and did only too late, new

money is a miracle
drug, though not
all cures possible.

While the world works out
on its treadmill
of invasions and buyouts,

the poor are left to tend
their luck that lack
of money lends.

For them, hope falls
between cracks in the boxed
bricks of the calendar on the wall.

Glut, not thrift,
is what we had;
now a glut of thrift

is what we've got
to start,
a way out.

The poor:
as if a dollop of dollars from
the rich would cure

empty hands reaching in,
craving even the curdled
butterfat of heaven,

as cries of the miserable are set
like an instrument to the lips,
to complete a circuit.

There's so much
dying still alive,
so much

to be extracted from the inner
circle of the latest lucky
lottery winner.

Too little or too much money
freezes
me.

For Christ's sake,
draw the string of the silk
purse of keepsake,

and in the measly stream of days, grant
a dirt floor for
the coming migrants'

home,
that the floor remains
somehow firm.

In the terrorism of money,
where dollars are at stake,
there is no democracy . . .

We know those who govern
are corrupt, since given the chance
we would be the same.

As the enterprise veers
toward its end, you have
no heart to fake any more

than you can outrun a toothache
through which the world keeps
in touch . . .

My young Filipina dentist looks
too small and frail to pull
a flower, let alone a tooth.

8—

This long, late, headlong
start of a running jump
landing

us where we are is running out
through a spigot old
as carbon, old as just about

sun-rays packed in the planet's pulp;
old as everyone
gone in a gulp.

It goes
away only with our going . . .
So, out of chaos

present and to come, you're here,
smelling roses
in the heavy heat of summer,

having lost most battles,
and some you could not tell
winning from *defeat*, as I can't tell

if this is poetry or penmanship, and if
I should switch when
opportunities for the greedy have

never been richer. Whoever eats
a steak, drives a car, flushes a toilet,
publishes a book, is in on it.

Imagine a face
resembling the lie
it embraces,

preferring to dish
its own given
gibberish,

yet how at the point of a pen
the flow feels
open in all directions.

Sure, there's much in the world to pity;
in you, self-pity had better be broken—
like a filly—already

in the homestretch. As death grows
more populous, each
loved one's loss feels new

each time remembered, a pang for a life
that lived its truth
to death, and now breathes slow grief.

9—

Wearing away
these
uneasy days,

close your eyes; gray matter turns
dark with what brain cells
of a lifetime have learned . . .

and between
two blinks of a bobolink,
a future plucked clean.

We are clods, schooled
by a god-
damn knave who makes the rules

and breaks them. Where
is the Assembly of Elder Experts
with oversight of the Supreme Leader

when you need them? If I could,
I would
brush God

with the tar
of living he has created
so far,

like the heart which heeds
only
its own needs.

No name
takes him
in;

no doubt
draws him
out,

nor the bellow and rancid heat
of panicked animals we
herd and eat.

Our eyes do not meet
eyes of the animals
we eat.

No plea or prayer
could a mind
prepare

for such a heart; no kiss
for such a humankind
as this,

spawned from a herd of cells
once
crystals.

Time to share in a long soul-
kiss—bone by bone—for each limb
to be whole.

Age is no thaw;
you don't get to go
but in the raw

from under the butterfly parasol into
the full bitter measure
of catabolic winds you have yet to know,

or, in fever, when you bathe
in the warm amniotic
waters of birth.

Recovered, you feel your powers in part
shrunken: one lung, one kidney,
half a heart.

Old age: hour
of the truth of poultrymen,
and the hen's last feather.

Toothless, one-eyed, in rags,
piss-stained, homeless,
grinning hag

on Market Street asks: "Wanna know
how you can be
saved? Yeah, you!"

10—

Sensing overload
of detail spreads
overload of dread,

I am trying to get,
as best I can, details of
catastrophe right,

of so incredible a sting
pulled off,
it's thrilling.

Riches, privilege, ocean spray
a passing gust
blows away.

What then about catastrophe
which—lived through—brings
on narcotic entropy;

or about having fun in catastrophe
makes it subversive,
and rejuvenates? Actually

fun finding what fits;
expanding, like oxygen,
the breathing of it,

while in our race
to eat the everything-on-it
planetary bagel before the mold does,

the economy works like a covert coup:
the military dresses in uniforms—
the economy, in suits.

Looks like the October surprise has come
in September:
Sara Palin, pistol-packin'

out of the tundra, seems the only one
having fun. Being chosen to
be unfrozen must be fun!

With luck, fun
can win; can offset
dour McCain,

but no match for the O-
bama-rama-righteous rumble rising
bile in peoples' craw.

Perhaps it will mean
a black man will live
his dream . . .

But, you were wrong before,
amigo: as per
Kerry, Gore. Or,

after hope turns to discontent,
will his disappointed followers perfect
a language of lament?

Such are things, I heard a woman at
the bank ask a banker, "Can you
make a living at it?"

When we withdraw before night
into our chest, our lungs,
our gut,

by nightfall, the desperate turn
back to mine the stones
from which nothing more can be drawn.

When a man or woman's name
is residue on the tongue
and must be spoken,

the lives war took
give themselves
back.

Then the sound of grieving
through a mask of gauze
is the measure of full receiving;

as gauze of shroud
blowing over sand
makes a barricade,

or a new class of warship poured
from the steel melted
down from the World Trade Center.

11—

Slung with automatics, semiconscious,
the hoary lords gather
their spent power at close

of summer, in the weighty air
of meltdown, and recede in order
to regain their footing for

the rebound, their bid to
renew dominion by subtracting
human need from their credo.

Their breath upon the sinking
temple mounted on gold bars
slows their falling

onto the slippery
edge from which slips
all safety.

Endgame: bar zero.
The statehouse brothel beds
the lawless retinue.

Could Bin Laden have wished
for a better ally
than George Bush?

I don't think so:
To have such an ally
as Allah who

wreaks havoc with the army,
wrecks their superpower standing,
and totally fucks the economy!

A moment when the light-
house beaming daily horrors stops,
and history lights

up. Bring a lens. Things in sight—
leaves, flowers, bell—thread-linked,
glint by day and grow by night.

And the whimper you hear
near the perishing
end of empire,

is bared
bones no longer bearing the weight
of the world they carried.

12—

As days dissolve
into depths in which
our lives are actually lived,

at night, in waters salty
as the Dead Sea,
you leave your century

to enter others happening
beneath, that have been
lived in all along,

as words spoken years before,
like the light of stars that exist
no longer;

light of a presence
as sole surviving
trace of its disappearance.

"So, light is the new dark,"
said Weegee, about Broadway
at night, in his car's back-

seat; he liked to work
alone, unnoticed, shooting
crowds, corpses, gangland wrecks.

13—

Will these weak days that can't speak
without confessing their emptiness make
failure complete?

Then, don't speak! Revere
less, mock more;
vulgar as vinegar, curse better.

What's gotten into me?
Is it powers
that be

who enforce
elemental
powers of a curse,

as when not
speaking for days
clears the palate?

Clarity? You want clarity?—
Be ready then
for clarity of night, not day.

Olivier, at seventy-five, about to play Lear:
"When you get to my age, with all
the nerves of your body, you <u>are</u>

Lear!" No one accompanies; the *you*
you call "companion"
is alone as you,

but for the instant that passes
between one person and another
when the space

between them is cleared
for the cleansing
of true feeling to appear.

14—

Clouds mass; thunder clears
its craggy throat. No sign of rain
on this side of the world; a rain of fire

on the other, as evening in the West
bleeds millions of bare feet to
dawn in the East,

where the song sung under a dome
descends the way sun in the last days
goes down.

The world's nations
work pyramid schemes on the treadmill
of principled invasions;

justified principles
outdoing in desolation
deliberate evil.

As certain words access
common powers
since they apply in all cases,

the hand holding power
forever holds a blank
check in the other.

Amazing that words still
have any meaning
at all . . .

Only when the work that gives
most pleasure begins
to determine our lives

can we count on more
colors in our rainbow
than we had before.

15—

The great hymn
from before home
had a name—

the wild planetary wailing,
incalculable suffering, each person
a world, misery prevailing . . .

The massed swollen hum
and gasp and choke of grief no word
comes from,

I first heard over seventy years ago in
my mother's wrenched sobbing
beside her mother's coffin in Brooklyn,

always here,
as though death were the air
that takes in the mourner

like an inn: stands
open and out
of which the future comes,

its velocity of change is
the secret
of surprise.

Whatever infinity
hands us of time, surviving
spends it the way

small
comforts we practice
draw a veil across the unbearable.

Old folks at Safeway, stepping out
of their isolation, look relieved
making chitchat.

Among women in Islam,
wailing is
no Poetry Slam,

but inherited lament,
defeat, dishonor, and more
of the same in the present . . .

A sound—heart-stopping ululation—as if droves
of birds' tongues driven wild fluttered
continuous glottal shudder, as in love.

Such wailing can peel
flesh off the hearer, lapped
in the lungs as a girl

wailing into
the endless open
emptiness without echo,

and fills
space with cries
more terrible.

The way certain past events
trace our talk
and actions in the present,

I'm beginning to feel a physical lack
I'll lament later, but now, lengthening
light of early September holding back,

dipping white butterfly wings
over end-of-summer buds
go dabbing,

and a Latina beauty in the Café Boheme
gazes long at her blank
cell phone screen

as if an absent lover
might discover the port he longs for
was inside the point of departure.

16—

In a turn from seeing
is believing to believing
sees, along

with Islam's wish
for annihilation and the peace that comes
with ashes,

Arabic script is writing
on the run, scimitar hooks on a wave,
fire leaping forward, driving

the past toward igniting future waves
in sweat-dots, a fire path driven
toward union with the absent Beloved.

A scythe people, minus crops; Berber
chieftain to researcher: "Raids
are our agriculture,"

where black gold
for blood is
bought and sold,

and only total destruction
of the visible brings
the invisible's resurrection.

17—

"Hitler bought off Pius XIII's Vatican
with a tithe from German taxes
of one billion.

Each year the Pontiff sent
birthday greetings to the Fuhrer:
'Warmest congratulations with fervent

prayers for you in the name
of the bishops and diocese in Germany
sent on their altars to heaven.'"

The orchestra at Buchenwald, the French
woman singing *Tosca*; fiddlers playing
for their lives by an open trench;

Robert Desnos reading good fortunes
from the palms of Jews
in line to the ovens.

Poetry had better see through the doors
of boxcars, or else not play
on the tracks anymore.

No more songs
to the balcony;
the balcony is closed. So long . . .

And to the new King of the Poetry Slam
I say, I'll see your Poetry Slam,
and raise you Islam.

O how many lands I'll never set
foot in! How many girls I'll never lay
eyes on! OK then, if not

in the same bed,
then in the same
world!

Handsome young man eyes
two pretty young girls
on the street, passing by:

"You girls married?" "We're not
even legal!"
"You got

to be kidding! You gotta
be out there so someone come
on to ya!"

18—

Wayward against the ways of the world,
or tight in its iron boot pushing
for a place in it by word

more than deed, have I let go by
what has the most
to tell me? Happens every

time. But there's got to be more
to go on
than what's already over . . .

Yet, as Holly Smith, the best
boss I ever had
at UC hospital, used

to remind his audiences
of stressed department heads, researchers,
Nobel Prize recipients,

"By the time you've made it,
you've already
had it."

And hope? Hope is having doubts
and thinking
second thoughts

about the present's beaten path
to what it continues
to have to put up with.

Hear, O heroes, the order
of preference by a prisoner
faced with torture:

*"Better a hundred mothers cry
than my mother; better
my mother than me."*

And the American POW, after
release from a VC prison: "I couldn't bear
unpleasantness, let alone the threat of torture.

Whenever I saw a fly
in my cell
I was filled with joy,

although I would wish for it
to slip under the door
to not imprison it."

19—

Tireless legs that walked New York,
Paris, Lagos, the Everglades,
don't care to walk around the block,

like the recluse Holan, for whom going
out on his balcony in Prague
was a rare outing.

Now going out the door
you never know
what you're in for—

sheen that feels substantial
in the air as an angel
turned animal,

or the body's hidden
wounds in middle age, bared
when old, in the open,

and each wave's white crest
is a calling
card from outer space,

with the last flowers losing
their scent, summer's
distillery closing.

Above the open, empty
loading yard
behind Safeway,

begins the long, unobstructed vista,
sky rolling out to the vast blue
rest of the West.

20—

Summer at rest:
stillness
of the stillest,

gulls hang glide a slipstream,
not a wingbeat stirs
among them.

The wonder in one
wing of all space travel,
and more than human

history in a feathered tip.
We know of no bird
consulting a map,

or how their song, momentarily
sweet, makes this world
otherworldly.

Then, as you pass,
a sweet scent like a new
thought sweeps the grass.

The princess tree you water
and watch breathe and gurgle
baby-bubbles at its base, and suck after.

And never far,
the Inuit's reminder:
"the weather is our master,"

and the drug-resistant pests
keeping abreast
of the latest

pesticides, to adapt
immunity from what's apt
to wipe them out.

Rest on the branch, little hummer,
before plumbing to sip the last
wells closing summer.

21—

In the West, a man
feels each beam of sunlight end
with him and with him begins

the long wait
for the unlit hour
before first light

while last light shimmers
in leaf-layered air
on silken wires,

until he sees in sunset's flash
the future of the heart
banked in ash,

and the stark
fires of bombed cities,
the new dark.

Freeways flow with dream-
lights, white and red corpuscles'
two-way bloodstream,

and the song sung to rest underground
descends the way the sun in the last days
goes down,

like investors seizing on the few
glints of less than terrible
corporate news,

which, going down the path of the possible,
narrows, contracts, deflects until the dead-
end inevitable deal.

They are like old men sweatily
in a steam room, luxuriating
in the tomb of their bodies,

while those working in mills, malls, uniform,
wait to suck their legal intake
from their trickle-down crumbs on the line

with no currency left but debt,
no value that displacement hasn't
demolished yet. And don't forget

the rejected, the evicted, the conscripted,
and the soon-bound-to-be
armies of the convicted.

Sad enough, you'd say?—
like some dimwit waking one day
to the famous fact his family is Mafia!—

while in a fog,
the world had defaulted
to hungrier dogs.

We are
old
dog behavior.

Y'all,
the kennel is
a-call-

ing to inquire
what it will take to change
an old dog's behavior;

to simplify the multinefarious and save
time since time is
what he doesn't have much of;

or get him on deck for departure;
it feels sick
ashore,

yet departure felt sick
when looking back
to shore from deck,

then dry-heaving sick
was the pits in the churning
middle of the South Atlantic.

Yet young,
unable to stay felt like a right
move to all that was wrong;

the way we go for diversion
to Art and are held
by the unknown.

The look in his eyes was made of everything
they had taken in
wandering;

even the seasons were travel,
without needing to go far
to see marvels.

He's white in a way much
like someone the sun
wouldn't touch;

and less
meant for sunshine
than a shadow is;

like a ghost humming
the latest thirst
for the same old nothings

worked on him in childhood
whose god keeps
his children good,

and like oneself will
hold on to the worst
because it makes him whole.

J. Ackerly had to decide, and did, to keep his cancerous
old dog Queenie alive as long as she kept holding him
in her gaze.

22—

Walking from hallway
to study, I lost touch
with my poem the other day,

or was it months since I put this down
and picked up again
to see what has gone down?

I have been mounting
an effort to outwit disaster
by keeping track, accounting.

Back when there was space and time
to grow in, it seemed a crime
for a boy's mind

to let a chance combination—often
collision—of words accelerate the
imagined at the speed of fission,

and then, for sanity's sake,
leave it as incomprehensible.
Those worlds that words create,

the original magical thinking:
beams straight from
a winking

starlit language
not yet known, not yet reaching
any page.

It was positively Kabbalistic,
if not already
gone ballistic.

Could such a language be—not as if,
but indeed—
a form of life?

And though I may
at times distantly wish to
conjure you . . .

O rid me
of the wasted
wish—immortality—for lately

I'm solely of the earth, in aging, reminiscing,
running back and revising, only to regret ignoring the plain-
spoken prose of those missing,

and that the unadorned may have held true
meaning looms like the once-distant
wail of a freight train barreling through.

Ah, the way mind works!
What in youth drove it,
old age subverts.

Nothing's mystical
in words after the physical
has run out; little

remains of a once dim or bright
light at the center of childhood
in the middle of the night.

"The poet in you wants
what he says to *matter*
to the man you aren't

because the poet wants
to *be*
the man you aren't,"

the way you want what poetry does—
not to live and die
in prose.

23—

Naomi, at her ailing mom's
in Florida: back, forth, back
next week, sure to go again

for the end that holds
on. Adults tending their parents
at the end return to childhood,

home. How come, young,
we connect
with end things

to the end of the line
before we have even had a chance
to have been?

"Not having children is sad;
having children is terrible,"
the grieving mother said.

Cut to TV: father holds grown son
with AIDS on his bed doubled-
over in terminal fetal position,

sobbing, trembling terror,
bear-hugged by spooning,
rocking father.

Schooled in instincts, fathers must hone
instincts
of their own,

for instance, surviving
by
lying

low. Set in stone. At your age,
celebrate Father's Day with a commemorative
brick at Brooklyn College?

Not so for the large
seaborne creatures whose clicks and moans
are no match

for sonar, no more
than silver-backed gorillas are
for pouchers' fire-power.

In Chechneya, captive children dying
from wounds, a mother asks her captor, "What
are you humming?" "I'm not humming; I'm crying."

"Such brave, innocent hearts" . . .
Notice how only the sacrificed
are praised like that,

while the most radical men are trying
to escape
the terrorism of dying.

24—

In Berkeley, I marvel the way
young mothers put up with their kids.
Relentless worry

for their safety should earn, say,
more than food stamps—maybe
combat pay.

And here, heavy older women lug
hips which younger women whip
making love.

In a woman's shrill
laughter, a startle about
to grow hysterical—

in it, present splits
to past out of
a choked throat.

What you would miss
if you got
your wish

for a lighter
load of love
to bear

is years together, two
heads on
one pillow,

eyes open
against a window.
When it happens,

folk of the future, forgive us, your
self-impaired parents
for the shape in which you find us here.

If you are here, after searching far,
forgive these gene-damned, God-depleted test-
tube babies among the stars.

25—

And too late
for your mother
to call you in from the street.

Dead and gone she is,
and all you mean to her,
mouthed to ashes.

Her question in Arabic "What's
in your heart?" you thought meant
your belly. You wanted to eat.

You have not, since then,
been that
hungry again.

All you know is, her part of you
you left, and her dishes
now you would grovel to.

And her roses
she hardly tended:
"Smell this,"

tilting a rose
as if she'd grown it
only for our noses.

Motherhood: 24/7 no matter what,
job includes a clause
that it can't be quit!

She wished the kingdom
that rest gives; going
unseen

despite what
keeps everyone moving
in sight.

Love's delayed sorrows come
in old age's late
rich ruin.

26—

Through blown hair
we approach
the touchy tips of each other;

soft focus,
soft caress,
cross

borders, when she gives you
those bedroom eyes
that see right through

you. Her mouth can blow
dead men
back from the blue,

eyes like pale
blue stems out of
workaday soil

of her makeup. All rinds,
ready to open,
in their time.

So what about moments that used
to flow and return
what happened to us?

Deathless, they died on a hill,
just as those mountains of wisdom
know less than little

of what to do when small
animals approach and begin
as species to fall,

like my sick kitten's slowly
lowering black liquid eyelids
growing visibly

old. How much pain
is open to whatever lives
in the weather we live in,

confusing, pursuing, continuing
like we had it
coming.

O mother whose wish
was for the sweet-tart
flesh of a McIntosh,

we're not asking for any bless-
ings anymore, just
a little *rachmunuss*

as our humming is threading
the needle of no return,
and spreading.

Pain
is the first
permanent lesson.

As you try to keep fit in ways
you never dreamed
you'd get sick of one day,

forget
the old bathos for the new
severity that gets

now so
meanly strung, soul-vendor,
mind-bender, singa

da song, compliments to
Gil Sorrentino, Joe Ceravolo.
Ciao.

27—

Among things I didn't know
I'd know until later—
which is now:

I remember, I remember
diving for depth
and coming up for air,

my mother's chintz curtains hold
an afternoon's quiet, suspended
in ironed folds;

her once telling me,
"If you love me,
leave me;"

and of going blind:
"First I see cobwebs,
then I see clouds."

In summer, when skin
is pressed as into
softened paraffin, then

lightness of body,
naked, made me feel
I'd blow away.

I had wished not to
have to wait
to get old before I knew

what the old know, what
I thought they knew.
It seemed like serenity, but

was senescence,
and their wisdom,
silence.

28—

December's grimy window days,
staring long and hard,
looked all the way

from storm and lightning-lashed
skies piled like a blacklist waiting
to be whitewashed

to May, today, when the wreck
of state is even less
haven from havoc,

with stealthy, sly
agents wielding less light and heat
than a firefly's

flash. But the nature of spring
on all things alive
is smiling, spreading . . .

On the surface, gilded ocean
peeling dog-eared foam
at stagey sundown.

From a palm, a swarm of butterflies
scatters like a meteor shower
in a red-rinsed sky.

O, if only the honey
in the precious pot, never ceasing to run out
of what we piss in, weren't money.

Out of the blue everyone draws down
in bowls held
with both hands,

feeling like weeping now,
the weeping
I'll have to do

later in this
only world that matters.
I've made a mess.

I wanted what I couldn't give—
the heart, time, and space
to more widely live.

If it's all good,
then how much more of this,
by God.

29—

There's a rainbow in my cell phone:
arching iridescent vapor
inside an airtight screen . . .

meaning longer days? shorter nights?
If we're talking spring, bring
on the long, indolent sunlight,

and on the stone path dust
like velvet
spray, sea-green moss,

for somewhere still a good thing
is coming in,
a labial iris beginning

again; sparrows breaking for cover
in the rain making their own
meteor shower.

One day they'll weave a house
out of wisps their beaks
pick from lint and gauze;

yet how human the sound
their curt, squabbling
snipes all around.

We, slowing down, pay closer
attention to high notes dropping
off and lower

earth-notes we bend
no ear to: tidal, temblor, tectonic
tones. Now lend

an ear to what's spoken
so that sharpened hearing
may become vision.

Looking backwards,
living that half of our lives
with the half that ages forward

in a dark familiar from repeatedly
getting up each night to urgently
pee,

one day we learn
we are mostly
made of phlegm . . .

yet somewhere still a good thing
is starting over: making lunch
in the kitchen, women laughing,

trills, thrilled as birds.
Each day you hear it
is good news in the blood,

like the songs we played
in the days of love
we made;

in eternity's nano-
bliss, as close
to the big bang as we get to,

followed by fresh-brewed coffee's
first aroma of the day: pure
alchemy!—as is

the rainbow in my cell phone's
call
I'm waiting on.

30—

Treading air like water at close of day,
wind in the face pitched headlong
making no headway,

went out to tie the wire-band tighter
around vine-limb and archway to hold
up the works we worked so hard

to keep from toppling, up
on its thin tin rickety
frame to bear the crop

of roses trailing scent
from some underground
Orient.

Clippers in hand, felt silence deepen,
expanding the dimension of time into space, and a voice
in the vastness enjoined:

"Don't lose touch with the garden.
Keep up my sapphire and sky-
blue lobelia as long as you can."

Hell of a job description
these down-sized days, if ever
I heard one.

We'll have to be lucky as some unlucky
fate gone wrong; as wasted nights recalled
now fill with song. And maybe

a time so contrary might
see things that have always gone
wrong go right.

OK, then, I'll take
the deal I'm driven
to make,

that, if taken up, would give the ill,
the terminally grieving broken-hearted,
a dwelling ground to till,

as when detailed
microscopic sight of botanical
rot looks beautiful.

How with the coming of spring
the earth seems to
remember something,

a stored force
released, driving
fever to the surface . . .

or is it the sales-pitch caller
from the funeral parlor after "taking care"
of a loved one, who inquires—

with embalmed empathy—how you are:
"We're here
for you; just remember."

We surely will.
We are the ever-renewable generational
ground they till.

In a world of slaughter, earthquake, flood, tsunami,
a quiet sunlit garden sits,
a lap of luxury,

and time turning silken
as in the arms of women
who know they own

what men seek
to own: now silken, now mercurial
key to the House of Sex

for open house,
upwrenching, spongy
sunrise in the phallus.

Her saying, about deceit and sexual jealousy,
"Marry a beautiful woman, but not
the most beautiful," makes her more beautiful to me.

"Can you get into more sex?"
I ask. "Go away,"she laughs.
"Is that a yes?"

"Next time." This time
I laugh at how desire,
wasted, is such a crime,

denying the chance for sexual glow,
attesting women's power
in saying *No*.

31—

"It's time to furnish your summer,"
says the ad. Thank you, my summer
is furnished, and a burner

to boot! Global warming? Hell,
how about fired-up old barbie,
and not in a Taco Bell shell

kind of way! How 'bout the mass-destructing
way Wall Street has
of self-correcting—

sharp as a hawk's talons above
a shrieking henhouse!
How far have we to drive

on empty
before we see them in the rear-view
getting away.

How full the workforce's
lunchbox is
of loss.

As if we each hadn't begun
to star in slow-motion
footage of extinction

to the last lethal still,
making it true our image
on celluloid kills.

Mid-May, just a tip
of the top of tropics, and a whole
Sahara of heat coming up.

How much must
such a killing heat have scotched millions
of species from the next

survival step! A friendly planet
this hot? Not, you'd think,
but for us. Go ask it

of Professor Irwin Corey,
The World's Foremost
Authority.

He knows bullshit.
Try him; he's an artist
at it.

We're not making up
for mistakes of the past,
we're making them up

again, as we go, like all
who need help from the ill
will of the unimaginable.

32—

Now a violet iris bends
from the waist
back in a breeze, then up, a wand

tracing a finger
along a curving figurine, following
her death from cancer,

like the cold water
taste buds
soak up, and just after.

What I saw
in sleep was no dream but replay
of evening news:

a slaughterhouse's concrete
floor, downer cow trying to rise,
blasted by pressurized jet

from a water cannon,
the hose aimed, engulfing
its breath like a dragon

full force at mouth and nose—
waterboarded—drowning
on its feet. I want the hose

turned to jet
on the man
aiming it.

But isn't rage guilt
for my part
in the kill?

Aren't we graves
of the animals
we have

eaten? And that smell, rank
lab rats in the hall
on my way to the office, the stink

growing stronger the higher
the stairs I bounded: caged,
matted hair, squealing terror.

From the open window crack
I'm crouching at, my pumped
Red Ryder aimed at the black

cat on the fence. Squeeze trigger;
cat drops. From behind, a smack:
"How *you* like it?" says my mother.

Either the world will save
you by drawing you
out of yourself,

or its hypocrisy
will drive
you crazy.

Save the whales! Save the ocean!
Save the birds! Save the world
in your spare time!

33—

Rilke, for the sake of a rose,
knit himself a trellis for
a new kind of caress.

Oppen: "I have fallen from the tree.
I do not know
what will become of me."

I know of no more succinct
account of the mind's terror
at going extinct;

of the animal we come from,
the panic in store for it,
scalped of illusion;

panic prowls the streets
and penetrates the heart
it dynamites,

like Céline's emotion
recollected more
richly in delirium.

Panic's troops: "Fuck with us,
and you'll soon smell the gas
that ignites the abyss."

I'll try to keep it in
mind, though there's more
"it" now than

mind. Here is your garden;
here is your burden.
Between sundown and dawn,

summer will be gone,
and with it generations of humans,
ground grain between grindstones.

And those disappeared from
air you breathe
while you can

are hooked in passing,
yanked to where
time and space are missing,

as all will
be, in the interstellar dark
night of a black hole.

Though today clouds
look in
a good mood,

I wonder how Hölderlin,
nearly forty years insane, wandering
in that good man Zimmer's garden,

would have sounded
knowing the winding river
Neckar below his window would round

back one day from the ex-Nazi Heidegger's
hut, where to his baffled guest Celan he'd say
not a word of shame or sorrow about the disaster.

Here is your burden,
here is your garden, here
autumn will arrive before dawn.

34—

Only days after high August
heat's hallucinogen, and already autumn
tints and rust-

red brown in leaves of the maple.
Summer's moisture, vanished,
bare feet slide smoothly in their sandals . . .

Now golden turns blood-amber
not like the outward ache of spring,
or a full table in ripe summer,

but the final irrevocable
sinking in of a season's full
primal measure we recall

like travel
that needn't go far
to see marvels . . .

just the peak of Mount Tam visible
above fog bank floats
on folds of a silken veil,

smoky white cradle
of a sea above us,
beyond trouble.

Each bare, winter creature
returns to its solitude,
small, cold, threadbare.

Some disappear without trace. Long after
our parents aren't
anymore, memory is our

parent. Nearly overcome
knowing the turbulence
coming on,

we try to salvage
what we can
of the spillage.

35—

Now hearing Larry Fixel, gone
yesterday, here
today, more quietly than

ever, quoting Eliot: "The powerful may not mean
to do harm, but the harm they do
doesn't concern them."

I wonder if "Possum," in his sly blend
of piety and subversion, might have
had God in mind.

I did, when Renee, near death,
hooked to an oxygen tank, gasping,
hardly had breath

left for the taking. Is it then
the past, for which we waste
the present on, takes on

a depth of sorrow
neither memory of,
nor future joy,

dispels? Then we're tied in knots
of loss and grief until
we're not

ourselves anymore. Only naked in a cage,
eye-level with an ant, could Pound's word
be trusted in despair and self-rage.

St. Elizabeth was his sham
coo-coo refuge from otherwise
certain execution for treason.

There are no more cries from the rubble.
Not a bad way to go: from feeling sleepy
to not feeling anything at all.

And how about the Air Force outfit
that flew defoliation missions; their motto:
"Only we can prevent forests."

Larry, in his orange sweater,
repeats: "Let me hear you,
if you're there . . ."

and he will
hear soon,
at his memorial.

Like a man at his peak
no longer needing
to speak—

not Elijah, Jesus, Isaiah—
let the slow, blush-rose
dawn, be Messiah . . .

But last night has lent
this dawn more than a hint
of darkness dragging like lint.

Without the sun,
we each go
into our own . . .

O Lord,
let it not be
more

than a day! And how about
this record downpour
preparing for decades of drought

to come, when Earth will be going
the way of wilting
planetary zoning!

Heavily spritzed are
birds, yakking up a storm
at the open-air bar.

36—

Ass in jeans do-
ing the wriggle
the worms do,

whatever beauty Art has
to offer better be a wake-up
call to witness, or else

it's landfill,
fluff; for the species, terminal
bluff, downhill . . .

It must be getting harder,
going
for easy laughter.

Comedy knows
no heaven
like rolling laughs;

laughter wildest
amid woe
severest.

But there are things so terrible,
to speak them
is to spread them, fatal

as the final
mountain in the mind,
mute, immovable.

A funeral
standing
still.

37—

Reader, let's share being alone
awhile: to think
outside the coffin.

Can what we desire
to exist be made
true? Or are

we seeking words
for the haul
into the wordless; words

which, before meaning,
come heavy with
returned feeling;

come to stay,
and only under protest,
praise? How

sudden as ozone scent in a thunderclap
after a summer shower peppers
the tarmac, then stops,

when you've had
the experience you wanted, and the words
for it are discovered.

How, threatened with disease we enter
our bodies,
blind strangers.

Is it all this which won't keep?
For instance, happiness,
for which we weep;

losing
a last hand;
and choosing

a way down
others have gone
and left behind

slackening ends. When they come,
you'll know because you'll have given
over your powers to them.

38—

Summer catches fire
at a touch
of daylight air,

and calls
its dandelion children
as they ripen and fall.

Yesterday is real
today in the stories we tell,
and the sound as well,

nearly unheard, like the dull
expanded thud outside the window;
rain-soaked, rusted cowbell

on a limb, hung
as if for a herd long passed.
You hardly ever hear a gong.

While summer wanes and autumn weans us
of sensations retreating
for warmth from the surface,

praise you've wanted said
of you is puffed
about the dead and near dead.

There he goes, with the gift of gazes
from young girls' glances
he now glazes

over girls who make Art
out of their you-
know-what;

and more than gold
on new grass, it's sunlight
on their tips he wants to hold.

And though he's won bigger
prizes, loud applause, he still envies
those who've won smaller

awe for the way
they sing what they had
to say.

While a cricket in the tongue shrills
to be wolf-whistling
like choirs of whippoorwills,

an early mocker in an elm chirrs,
chortles, then slides
off-key with such running racy humor

it puts to shame
the flat-footed run
called fame.

One bird, many songs.
Listen to one of the many,
and sing along . . .

In New York, on 3rd Street once, I met
Miles Davis. At how much I loved
Sketches of Spain, he spat, "Too sweet,"

and went on hailing
for a cab, yellow swarming
bees too practiced at profiling

fares on the spot to stop.
Rain fell; I left the fine-boned,
famous ebony features, thumb up.

39—

As a fever is to heat,
as a cheetah is
to speed,

as an electron careens
now here, there,
and in-between

nowhere, if for a few
hours you want diversion from
the dread and boredom of being you,

on the cusp of dysfunction
we get to ogle the net's dazzling
demon of total distraction—

mashup fragments bound
for fandom's hive-
mind in the round

where access to increase
of detail brings
on increase

of dread. Plenty of people are making
a good living retreading the market
sinking, war thriving,

and prices not to be believed
will be falling in fall
sales, like leaves

in cold weather
when maple leaves turn
redder, brittle, barer.

Autumn, too, trades
in subtraction—light,
blossoms, leaves, birds—

whose slow withdrawal draws on
the aggrieved wound
living in everyone,

and the old days
knocking on your door,
asking, "Can we stay?"

40—

What gives words power
is the past in the present
and a future they'd matter

in. When true words come out of you
in the moment
they come to you,

what is now
real lives
in you,

tested
against the most
that can resist it.

Self,
calling
attention to itself,

you believe good-hearted,
level-headed, compassionate,
and haven't even started

to break the back of each prize
notion and bring it
down to size.

41—

Lately my email is full
of news from friends
with illnesses that kill.

Sudden as a nosebleed, how,
anywhere, any time,
comes a blow.

The doctors have given him only
six months to live; he said
he could do it in three.

"I've lost so much weight,
should I buy new clothes
with six months left?"

No need to share our best
wishes, just results of
our latest blood test.

We've reached a level of stress
unsupportable at least,
and unacceptable at best.

Here's the deal:
choices limited;
chances nil.

"Green, green,"
I lobby with Lorca, "I want
you green."

All the green in view,
all within
a silvered bowl of blue;

green gone
to oil slick; green that is
the desiccated sand dunes' dream;

and hear the green
conglomerates preen
the future's Eden. Won't happen.

And though happiness may raise us
a moment and make ashes
look like daisies,

it's an illness
just aging,
if anything is:

becoming more of the whole
of what's headed
for a black hole,

along with the wholesale
slaughter of Tutsi neighbors the human-
hunting Hutus swallow like a festival.

42—

Each day you dole out
a dose of drugs
to wake, then knock yourself out

at night, just as you need your shot
of bad news
before your day can start,

and the world's foremost weather
forecast: wildfire
war

not only kills
soldiers and civilians,
but the children, as well,

that mothers might have had.
So a cleansed, altered future lives
in place of the childless dead.

Good men, in combat, will give
in to killing
in order to live . . .

You watch their eyes push-
pin into her silken dress
and penetrate thighs in a rush.

The mind mouths orders,
the muscles stay put.
Good luck with that, soldier.

With shadows in daylight that blow
your cover, you wait for sundown
to crop the gold of day.

The guilt we give
ourselves is a gift
that lets us forgive

ourselves in the ministorms
brains perform
time travel in, and summon

out of billions of cells
the very neurons that fired
the event now recalled.

I could reach into the present
if the future didn't keep opening
a sobering long-distance

view
looking
through

the heart of time,
which is a moment, over
in no time.

43—

I keep still,
and it comes—news
of the world, the usual

terrible. Where's it going? Spare
me the myth the mirror
sees there,

for memory is a house; in it, though
hardly anything was said,
time would find a way to betray.

More and more, in old age
grows a time
to put aside language,

and bowing
its limp
inch of wing,

love's weakness
gives in
house to house.

To tell the story would
be to set out
on a road

on which I looked for occasions
of the feminine for good
things to happen,

house to house,
giving in
to love's weakness.

What I see now is clear:
everything without
me here,

looking back from
where
I am,

like a dancer is used by the dance
and all the more
happy for the chance.

Near the temple
of melanoma, I'm here
with my white cells

before I go white
in the air
I bite.

44—

Today makes a week
of wildfires at the edge
of the continent: sky, smoke-

veiled; cindered air,
grit for sore eyes;
burnt timbers,

airborne forests of ash, dust settles,
rosy-hued pollution
over sunset more beautiful

for being more lethal,
in fact, able to be looked at:
wafer, purple orb, funnel

from which solar winds whirl
a foundry of rust, forging a
day dim only a little

less than the darkness coming on,
the horizon nightmare
for sailors steering for haven

and seeing risen
around a dome
swelling to open

whatever is to come,
and the heart puts aside
all hope of heaven.

45—

Everything crowding into
the present, to be first
tended to.

Poem, you'll have to wait;
my cats crowd the back door,
crying to get out,

but sense winter's
edge outside and do not exit
the open door.

They are
sphinxes
in fur,

after whose snarls and swipes, fur-curls
swirl
on the floor.

Why tonight I feel drawn to animals
in their holes, in thrall
to their hunted withdrawal?

It may be that look
on their faces, that have
the look

we once had. My ambition:
to make their litter box
a Zen garden.

What I say
to them I say to creatures
that look at me

as though talk was excretion
of the human, and
not worth consideration.

46—

Red November sundown horizon fades
in layered lightwaves, staggered
layered shades . . .

Night is aging into bloom—
leviathan-tentacled spills,
reefs, corals, shrouded plumes—

whose tar starves, drags down
deep-water creatures
in their own

element, sunk in
their suffocating
oxygenless realm.

Soon on the way, clouds
holding back rain
from famine and drought.

We, who get our peace
from its little faith
in good, and grow less,

expect the expected
disaster, which may hurt
less when you expect it,

as suicide trades up-front pain
in return
for long-term gain.

Meanwhile farmers of freedom manufacture
unimaginable misery for others
in endless wars

for increased market share in the unreal
that people have been fed
their need to feel.

For instance, before impact, a bomb
holds nothing
personal against anyone;

everyone's
fair
game . . .

as are we by living our way through
what feels like the species' bedrock
mandate to endure.

The information rushes
toward you
when you no longer judge;

when hidden intentions, oily
lubrications of the human voice
are worn away,

and a judgment is dropped,
eyes opened to
beyond where they had stopped.

Like for someone going out
after long illness, the heart forgets
how heavy winter limbs had felt

before giving way,
making ready for
April's autopsy.

47—

But, days later, hey, things have begun
looking up: the sky clearing
back to its usual pollution,

and you taking delight
again in getting details of
disaster right.

What is going on is instant
attention to absence
imminent.

Always dead ends ending up,
that must be exited
backing out, up-

ward. Places from which you
wished to be elsewhere
will be where you return to. . . .

It is there in heat
that brings you—
light-headed—

to your knees. In it,
off Matadi, to lie on deck
was to hallucinate

tidal waves and wrenching troughs, where
rushing rough-hewn blocks ground
granite groundswells under.

Time running out, energy low,
clear the deck
before going below.

48—

At this age, bodily weight beginning to rankle
most, pressures of a lifetime
amassed in his ankles,

his gait seems one
prolonged suspended fall
in any of many unintentional directions

he can't foretell, no less
control; treading, barely moving in air
as if water, breasting, in place.

All day indoors, he'll rush into sundown
gasping to taste the bronze on his tongue
of air not his own, or anyone's.

Sunrise, sunset,
beating
day's heart

in the service
of no one's
myth.

What myth,
he wonders, has he
come with?

Before he would have a future,
he'd go to the past—Africa,
which has no future

the fevered sun erases
any drive, or trace,
or any taste

for. Reckless young, he wanted to
be done with, over, and boarded
a bateau like Conrad and Rimbaud

up the Congo, massive, mangled
forest green curtain on each side, froth at night
cascading white down a torrent of tangled

roots, limbs—ripeness and rot. Nightly, corpses
littered the roads; noon paused its slather
of slowness for quickness in the dance.

The sun, a furnace-like vengeance,
reflected light's cruel, viscous, vibrant
quiver from every surface, ageless

cracked face like a sundial
without
a dial.

There, for the Crusoe of the heart,
world's end
is a fresh start,

the way orgasm sends
and catches us
up in the present;

the way screams of the spirit spit
for miracles
in the pit;

how ecstasy and exasperation
at flood stage will shoot
into words pure and urgent as they come

and henceforth belong
to the race as long as the race
longs in song.

49—

There were times he was sure
he'd give in; times
he was going under,

all the while
sitting shivah; always
a coffin, never a smile.

He is curious, obsessed,
about the moment when any help
will be of no use.

He has a theory:
we are in trouble—
where we should be.

Something tells
him there's no
hell

like earth, where it should be: quakes,
coups, tsunamis, epidemics. Is it fated
the poorest, weakest, hungriest, can't get a break?

He is relieved to hear Spain
apologize for the Inquisition.
No word from the Vatican.

Here, in California, the long
burgundy iris's first
sunlight-lapping tongue

opens to Arab Spring running riot;
bodies closer in street clothes than ever;
encircled, then ominous quiet,

and still the mass grave's moving
labored rhythm in spooky footage,
as if taken to proving

they're still breathing underneath since 1942,
before we had a clue collapsing species
are more like us than we allow.

50—

Might it be time in late age
for increased occasions to
put aside language?—

For the urge to speak has lessened,
and trust in words or wish
to be heard hastened

away like a dot
which grew and flowed and ends
in a blot.

He wishes the time he'd need to go through
in order to know this would be gone
through by now.

If it should prove good,
he has had his share;
if bad, he has had

a view: how blue lives
by never having
to arrive.

51—

The summer breeze, a dream of slowness
in slow motion's clinging
blue dress,

hovers like Pollock's hand
in the air from where
releases land's

light out of the far
or near moving
from there to here,

where money never sleeps
away a chance of killing
to reproduce for keeps.

Beyond our reasons
and us, lulling and dazzling
in deepening seasons,

sunlight's purpose—
to spread
happiness on every surface,

is always at risk
of its instant
opposite,

as when the bill for love
inevitably comes
due for grief.

The deep sadness that overwhelms
at parting and promises, promises
to meet again.

Quiet, please:
Death
in progress.

As the world's songs on the scale
of loveliness statistically tip
toward the female, meanwhile

a happy look, a woman's
laugh, ripe and resonant, stays
as long as we listen,

as when in work struck by the new
note that rings the true sound,
the false drops its garbage tow

away. You just have to listen
to hear it
lighten.

We did, and opened the book of the lost
voyagers who are at their best
when they are lost,

and not only able to leap,
but to build a bridge
back during the leap,

and a most beautiful boat
loaded with what spring
and its passing is about.

How we survived the incendiary
alchemy of Crane and Rimbaud
is a mystery, like the severe economy

and daring velocity
and bravery
of beauty.

Like the fugitive Dr. Céline's mockery—
manic, deliciously malicious,
pulping all Popes to pulverized piety,

and Nobel-worthy not only for literature,
he seriously boasted, but also for peace.
He was more

Jew
than he'd ever dream
he knew.

Come and gone,
the sun risen here
is theirs gone down,

age having worked
its numb
narcotic.

Quiet, please:
Death
in progress.

And those ambitions for a fame
even less than anonymous—
unknown—

fade and hiss along
with the day's evaporating
ebbing foam,

and the summer sky's vast
delicate thin distances go on stretching
unbroken blue continuing beyond us.

52—

Never have maple leaves looked redder
this late—
early December—

and though sixty-eight degrees may not be
global, it sure feels
that way to me.

But temperate California is nowhere near
the desiccate, stupefying
furnace of Lagos or Dakar.

After weeks at sea, a new scent,
floral, sweet mold before sight
of coastline: Cape Verde Island.

From there, for pleasure
in exchange for the horrors
the changing body is made for,

you sailed the swell
of women's
soft bell-

y fold, the dipping hollow
be-
     low;

momentary flicker
on a face, concentrated,
where no words are;

face almost forgotten, but not yet
finished being
looked at,

when the inner tongue of sex laps
body inside-
out, hauls the old, taps

the new plateau orgasm
reaches and goes
on from.

The new, for women,
is like the old
chance again

for genital flowering; dance
called
Romance;

and with such a glance
as yours that wants
all at once,

with not only the pleasure of seeing her, but
pleasure in advance, knowing
you are about

to, in summer nights that turn
women into amber spells; desired
flowers themselves that yearn.

Despite men's doubt, darkness, bloody news,
women's hearts set with genetic guile
on survival. O bless

their whole-hearted, hapless
stake in holding
out for happiness:

paradise
of sex,
with an address.

53—

She wanted to stun and kill
the world with her looks.
She failed.

She loved animals as a child,
and thought meat grew
on trees, like fruit in the wild.

What her mother told
her, she said, made her quit
meat for good.

In her mind, she has gone over
and over the scary
extent of her exposure;

sorrow came into her
eyes and filled them
like wonder.

From the Saigon War Memorial
Naomi phoned: "I feel like a Nazi
would in Israel."

Doesn't it wrench when
she says, "We'll be happy,
soon? . . ."

Just then, the concert
struck up on the ivories
and the whine of catgut.

54—

Your insistent darkness
pressures her
to light that darkness

in self-defense, she said.
You force her, fighting, into
the light, for which she is glad.

So in the passing speed of each in order
to return with more
of what is alien to the other—

there's love? There is, if our fate
is to be tapped
and resonate

when darkness nears.
So put aside
some sweetness for

looking back—no matter
how many years—that
its look stays clear.

How she put more colors
in your rainbow than you
had before;

how her breath can blow
dead men
back from leaden blue.

55—

At eighteen, I stepped
out of the solid world
underfoot into liquid

flowing surface, not knowing
toward what
I was heading.

Once, in Abidjan,
the sky, pink and blue
broad-banded sundown,

shimmered with new light,
as if from the other side,
dawn had been lit,

soaking through. A rain-
bow rolling light, rolling eyes,
dawn pressing sundown.

As, often able to see the beauty of where
we once were now that
we're not there,

all rinds ready to open,
harbor, seascape, crystal ball
sun you go down

heavily, and know
in your lucid sea-legged gut
you would follow

sundown and long for dawn. Now
rush to the top-floor window
as the sun descends, or be a no-show.

Catch the last rays,
and feel you've had some
part in the day.

56—

In these year-end holidays,
lovers are hardest on each other, and I
don't mean in a good way—

the way teeth marks
leave tracks
on bared necks,

or a look that passes
between one and another
when charged space

between them is breathing
the truth
of shared feeling.

Because only half
the world is seen
by oneself,

when two bodies see
what's been invisible
between them, and find a way

in the heat
of discovery
lying together in the night

to see clearly, the news
in alternating moves
animate and remake love anew.

Newlyweds don't have a clue
what those long-married have given—
feeble or fumbling—their attention to.

Now let us try,
says the rabbi,
kosher adultery.

As eyes of the old surge
back in their sockets and sink
to bone for refuge,

with Ash Wednesday's thumbprint on
forehead, the old woman's crinkled face
looks more ashen

than ashes; still,
a grain left
of a girl,

and a stillness of something
inert as it is
falling.

57—

(in memory, Morton Marcus)

Fog-shrouded February barely gone,
and with my first steps out,
a powerful scent-driven

blossoming springtide knocks me
squarely on my kneecaps,
nearly to my knees.

My friend has died; he appears
walking away in a sky
not there before

he occupied it
and now
inhabits

alone:
empty sky, no sun,
procession-of-one

returning a sum,
debt most
unforgiven, called in,

totaled. In moments of crisis,
as heart's submerged need springs
to surface, new eyes

see such a prickly pair
we were—yoked,
bickering brothers.

Yet how unstinting his generosity
rivaled in richness
his full-throated rhapsody!

If poetry is near able to say
what's not heard in speech,
perhaps he'll hear what I didn't say—

here, in out of the unbound
stretch and reach and touch of
time in sound.

Mort, we should switch places. Have
you noticed how those who love life least
often live

longest? Such a circus!
Applause these days
would be white noise.

On the phone, you
could barely whisper
you were ready to go,

though you'd breathe easier
if the world's cries gentled for the night.
You'd be elated, you laughed, near

healed, if drawn
out of midnight and daybreak's gray light,
dawn's pink palm opened.

58—

(Cataract surgery)

On your back, looking up out
a cloudy lens as an ultrasonic steel tip
pulverizes and disperses it,

crystalline shards uncouple
vision's wavelengths in color-cubes,
peel and sail

away like astronauts from the mother-
ship we see by. Light, gone
not dark, but white here

where sunset west
this hour comes
to rest. . . .

With an implant and wrap-around shades, I let
Naomi lead me onto the careening
glare of the street,

when near day's end, most
illumined, light rests
in the eye that loves it best.

An amber ray beams down a peeled
birch trunk and rides
a stream of gold

moments before dipping
over the horizon, like a bather
onshore, pausing, inching, giving

in. When injured, and we enter
our bodies, tottering
strangers,

the distance from events
that mean most to us grows
smaller, intimate;

and maple leaves never looked redder,
and weather was never warmer, and light
never sharper, this late, first of December.

59—

Ah, I see, evening prayer got
us to stand and bow and rock like a sail
in a storm before sunset;

a breakneck race
that passed for prayer
in God's house.

These days, just looking good
is a mitzvah, giving hope,
taking courage, refreshing mood.

For this,
men's adoration
and lust

travel
the distance between
surface and soul,

mental equal
of *kalpas*
in space travel.

A moment not harassed,
hunted down,
is a moment in paradise.

So while you stand in the sun
and feel waves in you swelling
to a farther one,

comes a moment's urge
to throw overboard
all ballast as purge

for what will give
unfettered ride
on reckless waves.

For those who travel
to enter distances
which imagination has held

back and find more than imagined,
a horizon remains beyond
our intentions after we've returned.

In the hard anchorages of rock,
we're going on
strings of instruments plucked

like skirts and blouses; like the wind-
vane on the roof opposite: Snoopy's four arms
spinning kiddy Krishna, nose downwind.

Overheard at Costco, by the meat department,
sales woman to sampling man: "Are you married?"
"Divorced." "You in denial?" "Replacement."

60—

Seaward morning in the mood
for miracle, grab sight
of a wing, upturned, wide-

open sky, where horizon's
edge bends
endless blue dome—

pale, porous hue
which all that is matter
passes through.

On my desk, the sky-blue cover page
of a notebook, 1994, faded
white around the edge,

a cloud's peephole,
upward, the whole
turning pale,

faded as a wish that winter
not be visited on spring
coming on. Make it far:

cold, wet, late
winter not finished
with us yet.

Low above sunlit telephone pole,
black cloud stacked behind brown cloud
in blue sky, Rothko sails,

as if a wind rose
in late day in a house
long ago closed,

and the garden cut back in autumn,
in December, all
thorn and skeleton.

Though light closes
in winter tight
as a rose,

and time touches
what light
never reaches,

where flowers were,
and the weather
was ours,

home is a bloom away,
where sun just set
on New Year's day.

61—

*"Words ring hollow in a well
of silence . . . Words wound,
silence kills."*
—MALCOLM DE CHAZAL

. . . Then what the hell, why not spell
out what there is
to tell, as well

as loving someone
past the time of lust-
flushed first attraction—

a person like yourself, it turns out
as cagey, capricious
as lust is universally hot.

Today feeling a happy day
in the midst of dread
days that don't go away,

like last-lit sundown rays
that tilt a lengthening stilt-legged
shadow in your way.

It would be nice if the blow you fear
would not have a chance
to occur;

if the mounds of moss between bricks
this early mid-January
were virginal, pubic

promise, unlike poisoning the sky
turning out to be our primary boom
industry. Our pie

is the sky, infinitely expandable,
expendable dumpster. And planned
human devastation, collateral animal

extinction, stay news
despite what dear Doc
Williams of Paterson says; stays

even days when horror happens
without headlines; ghost-grief's
shadow that spreads and stains

the heart in the hospital that is winter
depleting our bones in the high delicious
warmth, the sauna of summer.

So, sing, lifted note,
or fading
I'll forget . . . yet

still amazed that bees can remember
faces if they're tricked into thinking
we are strange flowers . . . .

We are; have also known
winds that crop
with WMD propulsion.

We are: brown yellow white black . . .
and once red,
but that was back

before they were rooted out,
penned in desert holes
to convert and rot.

Before another reign
of ruin is born
full-grown,

let a garden grown
long in full-
focused sunshine,

and the chromosomes of sons'
and daughters' however enhanced
beauty yet to come, become

what Naomi calls, "the new
improved model."
But I don't know . . .

It's a tall order when war—
incessant, unsparing—makes
children smaller,

Iraq, Afghanistan,
Somalia, Congo,
Gaza, Yemen, Sudan . . .

And, hey, Haiti's people—
Earthquake Art: piled
bodies in the streets, murals of rubble . . .

into which steps Papa Doc Duvalier
off a plane, thirty years "abroad,"
to reclaim his share.

Where's the light
that supposedly does not stop
at night

when the sun goes down but reaches
the deeper ground its phantom
particle energy enriches?

Why, on two feet do we wobble;
why does doing good
bring trouble;

how, in mugging earth's sore
resources, new money manages
miracle laws

that blow the tops
off mountains
for their crop

below, and make all
wars
justifiable

on fields of new flowers
holding on before the launch of spring
offensives, and just after, so far . . . .

62—

Might starting from chaos and on
to confusion be
a direction

for creating what's not been seen
of what is, and will—
in a blink—have been?

If an infinity of universes are
stacked like pressed pages
in a never-

ending book, an infinite number
of versions of *you* are
living an infinite number

of alternate lives in realities
playing all possible
and imagined histories,

including each series
played out in reverse,
and simultaneous, with ours.

Then somewhere, there's bound
to be George W. and Dick Cheney
hunkered in a hole in the ground,

any hole will serve as a mini-Pentagon,
with none of the comforts of a safe house,
nor new face in witness protection.

In the distance, a wail-
ing, warning
freight-train whistles

back to that factory I once passed; a mob
of workers exiting at twilight; the sign:
A sky without smoke means a town without jobs.

63—

Emotions have their seasons,
and seasons evaporate along
with our emotions.

Though some long-term catastrophe
may be igniting a lovely
short-term spring early,

birds in the trees cheer
it nevertheless deliriously
on, not far

behind, their
wolf whistles warming up
space with light and air.

So what's all this whining
and baleful barking about
"seeking" and "meaning"?

Who bought the winner's purse
at auction, paying more for what's won
than it's worth?

What if, when cursing life
and wanting to be nothing,
nothing *is* most yourself,

the way spring rain in early May
eases and warms
what it melts away,

each pearly
drop
a Buddha's belly.

So move it on, get along
little doggie,
get along.

64—

Summer hayride-wagon's
sundown on the way,
molten horizon's

bonfire obscured
by cordite clouds,
funereal barbecue . . .

Pray?—No way is Eden
coming
on,

for experience shows you
can get sick from a steady diet
of daily news

cooking 24/7,
money-powered
profiteering off human

and animal pain; raping
the climate for long-
term reaping,

capital's kit-'n'-caboodle kaput, and we
thrown in
for free; we,

along with the litter
we leave behind
where we loiter.

The bottle of pills
will fall
and spill,

the medication
will finally do
you in.

My friend, hakeem Sam Hamod, more
than a doctor—
a healer—

knows pain
is our Zen;
concentrated heat-beam

through a lens under
which wriggling down
we smolder.

Yet just to kneel
and bow five times a day would
make my nagging backache hell,

and here he's telling me of his triple-bypass
with *more* gusto (if that's possible)
in his voice

after coming out of it
than before going under.
A miracle, I admit.

He laughs, knowing I'm not a believer,
and goes on as if he believes
I were.

Seeing is believing,
so they say, but these days
seems to me believing

sees not only what the eye can trust.
He raises his eyes in gratitude,
Hamdallah, for all of us,

and makes a case—
whirling Sufis spin in dizzying orbits beyond
all sundowns with nevertheless praise.

65—

Having reached through growing dark
the age inclined
toward looking back,

rest now in moments when safety was
with those who wait for you
in days you lived together; whose

time, while present, flew
trains to Coney Island filled with summer's
human freight on rails below.

Shielding their eyes from the future's glare,
allow them ease, allow them laughter
now retrieved, that you hear

around the table it hastens from,
a resonance which lessens
as you crane to listen.

Craving mind
craning
toward its kind,

how sad: happiness
that needs
practice; happiness

that needs creating. For I confess
a laughter that did not happen,
a happiness that never was . . .

but each year a feature less
remembered: his set, whiskered jaw;
her guarded anxious

bunched furrow
pinched
between brows.

Instead, I see their weathering
reach my eye
through what's left from their withering.

Love takes stepping into a current
and resisting the rush of natural
self-interest, our primal parent,

and openly let ourself go
in an opposite direction, like salmon
upstreaming a falls to lay their roe.

Now the counterflow
to leaving them for somewhere
in the world I had to go

returns me to where
once were those who are
no longer there. . . .

Or am I, in turning at last
to a vast empty emptying open
book, coloring in the past?

66—

No Johann Sebastian Bach,
you call this
mock

cracked
rag-tag hullabaloo of
a mess—music?

After creepy, weepy Mahler, Stravinsky,
Schoenberg, Ray Charles's "death tempo,"
are we ready for Schnittke?

"I put down a most
beautiful melody, and suddenly
it rusts."

Hot, like the latest pop star,
for enlightenment, I too have squinted,
subilluminated, in the candle-light of the Zohar—

the Kabbalah's magical
algebra counting all
things equal.

Even so, time's sea
chafes and scrubs
the mystic out of me,

and breaking news from the siren street
is playback from long ago,
now obsolete,

unlike the Schubert
D Minor Quartet, or
the purring of my cats.

My brother Natie and I, catting again:
Sharon versus Arafat. He hangs up; I call
back. Blood is thicker than brains.

67—

Having reached an age
closing in
on the limit of change,

add to expenses
a steadily encroaching
foreclosure on senses

when sight recedes all around,
and a moment's presence is
delivered by sound

needed,
like the synthesis of light
inside a seed.

River flowing seaward,
and silence of the dead insistent
on staying dead,

let sound that has found its true
savor pass the feeling on, even if only
for the time it's passing through.

Goodbye in the sky,
wild geese cry;
goodbye through the window I

look through. Soon I
will have said goodbye,
abandoned by allies.

How unnerving to discover late
what you thought important is no more
important than what you thought

not. How I sometimes say
the opposite of what I think,
and think opposite to what I do;

don't you? How, losing the thread
of what you'd thought you'd see clearly, you scorn
the very words that once stirred

you for reasons just
as sound and likely
wrong as all the rest.

Turn to the mirror: the caught
sight of your pallid
likeness hurts,

while sound bubble
afloat on an o-
boe's warble:

sweet, sweet, sweet,
chimes early bird in a tree. Word
not yet on the street,

but spring better be! Near,
all it takes is a solo recital
by the white-stripe-winged mocker's

one-bird-band's chromatic scale—
the whole speckled
spectrum of birdcalls!

But this winter,
with its worldwide waste-
paper breakups, portends disaster.

So may the best
of God's blessing be
upon you, not less. . . .

How postmodernly odd,
in less than twenty years
Google is our God.

68—

Woken from the ways
of night, but not yet
to day's,

have you never had to
do the unforgivable
in order to go

on, and rerun back
a moment
before catastrophe struck?

Growing old a long
time now, longer than
young,

carries a weight
of past sun-
rises, sunsets.

To see an old man far off
in thought before
he makes a move,

is to see him
and not know
what holds him,

is hearing from bare
lips
there

no more to speak.
It gives an old heart
a steady ache,

tightens and loosens
its grip as it goes
on down.

What use regretting a bitter deed
you made happen once, over
in a heartbeat?

The chaos of the close view,
volatile as methanol you can't breathe,
though you're about to,

is like sugar buttons poised
for the sweet tooth;
and in the voice

stanching distance and dispersal,
you wonder if you'd better be
running with the animals,

running for cover
when the ban on the hunting season
is over.

69—

At Gettysburg, two musket balls—
fired from either side—collide
in air and fuse as they fall,

with cries of soldiers that swell—
war or no war—
for a mother's wail,

in the split-second wound
at its highest
level of pain.

Home
is sunset,
and the time

of such a house (at best
a darkroom), as always,
past.

We're moving away;
and those who stay,
stay

fused in the instant's
passing. That membership
in a moment

is not barred to anyone;
once, alone, soon
in the company of everyone,

as a petal in October will
join the mass grave
on which it falls.

70—

Older, slower
going, coming, returning
sexual pleasure,

and sharper,
with hot flashes
from the melting glacier.

From engorged phallus—
slow, so massive a feeling
grows, pleasure to the core, sunrise

generating ever-widening horizon,
until, detached, we plummet,
driven from then on to return.

Now dim winter sun, cipher
of its blazing in blinding
mid-summer,

the only yellow in the sky—
lemons on the branch, and sharp
as sunlight after surgery,

a darting rainbow-winged hummer's needle-
bill at a blossom
holds still,

as if at the end
we enter the full reality
of our intent.

Meanwhile, feelings come in tempos . . .
Vivace, Fuga, Allegro, Largo,
and the hammering ostinatos

of Bach's harpsichord concertos
like the dappling duo
tabla players in San Diego—

their tireless fingers would play
bodily all over each other, all
surfer-blue-eyed day

long. The longer they'd play,
the longer
they *could* play.

For some, no stop, only lulls
from buried
cluster bomb shrapnel;

from one standing in line
at checkpoints who turns
explosive, then into headlines;

or those who, in a healer's eyes,
see serenity assured, cure
personified.

71—

Daft, dumb, dear
star-kissed
past and star-

crossed aftermath, try
seeing
with doctored eyes

what's left
of our withering, and the weather,
lord willing, lift.

Why else the faster
depleted forests gulp
our carbon spew, the quicker, thicker, taller

they grow? Go
figure. Shoot a gun in the last standing forest,
and watch, lo!—chlorophyll eat and swallow!

Perhaps we'll discover in ourselves such unknown,
unimagined ways, we'll look
on ourselves with admiration

that, in more ways than Schubert,
could break
your heart.

Of the wind to come, even
a back-breath of scorched carbon
bubbling out of the blaze and babble, beats me down.

I have lost my instinct in the mounting
effort to keep hold
of calamity by counting.

Having gone from being able to tell when
the dead were present to wondering
if they had ever been,

I keep still, and still
I scatter; I work to keep
from weeping, and weep still.

As a cloud before a setting sun
lifts and makes it appear
just risen,

a world diseased of us
still bears seasons, and traces,
creases,

incised in one's
face in
a lifetime's expressions.

By sundown, the horizon takes in
rift and theft of everything dear
into the ocean it returns from.

72—

Long out of youth's lust-flush
and middle age
stuff-crush,

having to blink away a blankness
and smoky unveiling, as in
the onset of blindness,

you're looking at things and know
seer and seen
wiped away.

Old age has no aftermath,
but—deep, barely rippling the surface—
secrets holding their breath

for the crisis that brings the heart's
submerged allegiance rushing
to the surface, like skid marks

of the mighty, moneyed master-
molecules colonizing
human nature, like cancer.

Eyelids lift in outrage
at the laws they've had
to live, the banks to mortgage,

while pangs of famine go viral,
and deserts feed
on bloated entrails.

Perhaps someone will
have already summoned a time
more in touch with the invisible,

like batty William Blake's
ink-blackened fingers in service
to his Prophetic plates.

In America's declining age,
green no longer reaches
to the water's edge.

Jehovah-Allah-Holy Ghost-goo, God
is one "o" short
of good,

original spark
before beginning's
black

that calls you
back
from the blue.

The cold, desiccate blackout abyss
which hurtles the mystic back for want
of the warmth of an animal kiss,

brings on a fear
that makes you feel like
vomiting tears.

Yet quick as a coffin maker's hail
of hammer-blows
on a nail,

sunlight's purpose
is happiness visible
on every surface.

If evil were the least bit
merciful, death would hunt
down and kill it.

73—

Now past the age of active ambition,
a time comes like autumn's brief
burnt surge, gold-leaf flaming in the open.

The slow, low-lit end of day
spotlights things in one long beam
before they fade,

and like the aging lust
for the girls going by is
lust kept alive best

with makeup and lipstick, autumn
hoards dimming light, blossoms,
leaves, birds. Everyone

is in their late period and tells
in plain style their end tale:
imagined peril proven real

as the smell of holy smoke
in the stench of salvation's
moneyed speech in public,

and greed, graft, lobbying remain legal
under federal law, and the NRA's fingers
grip like tits the talons of the bald eagle.

Before the future allows
misery to be done with,
must the present's health grow

more pale with that long, steady stare
you see of helpless pitying, which one
creature gives another

on seeing it in mortal pain?
Ill, old, slow enough to take the moment in,
we'll go through this again and again,

and the countless in crises at home
and abroad, bedridden bodies warred over
by drugs and pain.

Out of things done or undone, I
wonder, of what I knew then, what
I would have done differently.

But it's too late for the done
demolitions and wildly fulfilled
deeds in the past to be undone.

If wishing is certain
to make it
not happen,

the way to go is not to wish at all
or want this kitschy Turkish dish
of delights that is sprinkled with gall

always at the point of maximum
stress, each cascading moment newly
arrived, tumbling off rungs

like seraphim seeking asylum,
frail, fading, or flickering alive,
hell-bent on the present.

74—

Too old to hate almost
anything anymore, everything
looks as good as the rest

to his Atlantic eye
underneath
Pacific sky,

but conditions on the ground such
as those calling him back to fading
black from translucent blue are a message:

on two feet, we wobble;
doing good
brings trouble.

Such revelations grind
and can raze a man
to a grain on command,

or he learns the lobbyist lesson
of using money as legal bullying's
terrorist weapon.

See him smile
as if tickled
by fate's sickle.

See him try to cool the close-up solar
heat rays bubbling red
futuristic weather . . .

Real stuff
out of
make-believe:

a used word
already half-
way there,

halfway to substance
in the flesh
and circumstance,

like a curse spun out into time and space,
whose vibes, however far, reach the target
moment they merge in time and place,

and stretch
the tissue between then
and now to living touch.

As for the many hidden truths
the heart has not spoken
to the mouth,

don't take
him off
his junk

diet of words and wounds
in the wind's teeth that blows them away
like footprints.

The mark
of quickness is to ride
the first spark,

as catching a glimpse of one-
self apprehending
a new perception;

or in the middle of music, the ones
aware of the magic
going down

are active agents
happily hurrying
the future's current,

as their features hasten
to the center of their face,
bright, excited, sudden.

In the light, shapes, colors, mingle;
the dark is a solid, glacial,
single

flowering tree
lit
with astronomy,

and undersea,
pulsing jelly-
fish glowingly

parachute out of a wide
open western
sky-

blue looking clear,
boundless, having to make
do up there,

while he's glad he's alive
and wanting to have the gladness
survive.

75—

Our eventual not being here
infects the present
in which we are,

and at times, a brightness flits
across a sunset's scroll
in which all lives evaporate,

and late in life
a pang of joy stops you
on a pang of sorrow, as if

in the midst of happiness,
you're reminded how
much you'll lose.

Perhaps it's because the part
you play you play
so well, hungry heart,

as only hearts can be
whole-
heartedly heartless, like the sea . . .

with gleeful spite
getting details of catastrophe
right.

Such delight
in crises and convulsion wants
to see the world prove it right . . .

Let the god-
fearing who pray like pleading
children playing dead, bury the god

they await to no avail,
and his still-awaited
miracle,

more dead than alive,
in flight from a cave, ending
in a cave.

76—

The way a Siberian tiger's coat grows
lighter in autumn,
anticipating snow,

I'm nearing a time
I'll grow lighter and run
out of rhyme . . . .

John Clare, here's to your everlastingly
being randy, and your cure:
opium and brandy.

Better to fumble braille-babble of the heart
than leave a gasp deferred
for death-bed regret;

better residue,
echo,
resinous clue

of a summer heat lying
heavy in the street; of a house
breathing kitchen smells and fraying

scoured surfaces inside
the window of a stilled world
that abides,

as in summer, when
torrid heat presses bodies
into soft paraffin.

77—

Reader, if you've endured
my yen for deserving
your eyes and time and future,

along with the gristle
and smell of
a cornered animal,

let me tell of gifts,
unrecorded in the record books,
that make our pensive natures lift,

as when deep in his groove, a pitcher's center
rocks low to the ground, springs and hurls,
a coiled whirling arrowed dancer;

or the succor
in the ebb and pull of one living
thing on another;

in the curvature of space, the rosette
ellipse a planet traces
after centuries in successive orbits

of the sun, and stars
scattered far,
are driven farther

apart in light years than dotted bean-
specks flecking a dish
of vanilla ice cream.

We live in an ocean of primordial light,
in which matter's thin
debris floats

and foams universes
in and out of existence in
ragged randomness;

our spiral
out of a cosmic dust storm
whose possible

source, Red Rectangle
Nebula, 2,300 light-years away,
whirls like a Huichel

woven core burning off layers
of gas and forming a cocoon
around its center,

as galaxies spiral on,
slow-motion
frisbees in head-on collision.

Hats off to the Sombrero Galaxy, its domed
white core and thin black
spiral dust band.

Moving out in space, back in time,
we approach, as to gradual sunrise,
original dawn;

the whole outrushing cosmos,
one blinding fireball;
everywhere core, infinite furnace.

78—

The beginning breathes out
with increasing velocity
to suppose that

all there is expands
hot birth to
heat-death's end.

Together, all colors
of the visible spectrum blend in
white's dolor.

To understand, then, is
to *not* make sense.
Our star's sisters

flee their carbon brothers
bound for broke; molecular
or massive, more miscreant than Mars.

Emptiness far
away inside ourselves
recalls Earth's rare,

imperiled atmosphere, premium
perishing sustenance of
living systems.

Meanwhile lurching
days roll out and in, checkered
as childhood's awning,

and the one who remembers, told
he is aging, still looks out
of childhood's

eyes. The boy who returns
is mistaken
for a man.

You asked for your childhood—
it has come back. Maybe it has
not been useless, growing old.

79—

It's your boyhood
watching
from the foot of the bed . . .

the clock-radio in dark
radium night glows
in solid black.

Shrill alarm, slap back
down; the same dark gone
to sleep in, there when you wake.

What knack or sorcerer's act
draws you that
far back?

It—if not all—now seems luck:
Nat King Cole crooning "Nature Boy,"
silver-fox-throated on a slow track. . . .

Then, how quickly, more than
a photo: smoky video, or slow-mo . . .
swing in the park high, high up I am

swung by my father in his business suit
and tie. Blond Sunday, blue sky
as ever, mute,

including sunshine, then shadows more
like ragged works-in-progress, which night was not;
its slow leaden noiseless pressure,

steamrolled pitch-black,
would spread and stamp
dimension, thin as a dime, flat.

I see him, the day, the light,
but it recedes without color, edge, or smell
of outfield grass, the early morsel of late

I chow down, as if the sweet ruse
lets me relight nerve ends
time and gravity ground out. This

happened; I was there,
some mote of me I carry
must care.

We didn't say much.
There was light, there was air, and
at last, rushing farthest at the backswing, touch.

80—

And what's all this chatter
about shedding new
light on dark matter:

inert, unknown, invisible, giving no
light, held together
with gravitational glue?

And how 'bout those binaries, that by twirling,
prevent (at least delay)
star-collapse, and keep things

stirred. What's all this inner whirling
about? Don't tell me it's another turn
of the self's Lazy Susan. It is, darling.

Star-soup's on!
From Red Sea to redshift's
Great Wall snuff-storms,

galaxy nurseries swarm
like fireflies in a summer night
twinkling above a hen-

house shrieking with talons.
See the beetle on the bark,
asleep there in the moon-

lit air. We'll have to drive way out of gas
to get on
in the universe.

Eros of endurance, don't move
from where you've planted
yourself, trunk, limbs, leaf.

81—

In a time when old men's needs begin
calling
on depleted means,

it's enough having control
of your bladder, and then
losing it, or rosy stool,

to make crystal-
clear your place in the lifeboat
leaking red corpuscles

and white leukocytes is—
like everybody
else's—

right here
with us who are
neither rich nor rare,

but common and complete naifs
plugging away
under Bosun Grief,

before the instant
change comes
and goes the distance.

Nobel candidates, please, a favor:
email fax FedEx text tweet
twitter whatever,

but tell me when a telomere's tail
begins to grow—not shrink—
in the aging cell—

(such tiny fins
infinity
spins!)—

on the way to wings
and gossamer
hovering

over
shadow of loss
that covers

everyone: aged
hearts sorrow has
time to enlarge;

weight-worn faces
carrying their entire body's
freight; lovers who embrace

lips aflutter,
sex
forever,

and look
to fix
on a hook

in space features
of a held face
before releasing it to a future

which can use a few
more strokes of true
justice, is hard to argue.

For instance, the bagged rabbi's mail
henceforth rerouted from shul
to county jail;

the hung corpse of Eichmann,
fed to the oven tended
by a survivor of the crematorium.

82—

In a world hollow with holes
underfoot, and underground riddled
by invisible moles,

we on the surface love on
a crust,
molten

underneath. O hapless ass
pulped
anonymous,

may you not come to believe chance
accidents mask elemental forces
aimed with malice;

or that for you
to speak your heart's desire
makes the opposite come true.

Let finger's
touch be slow, sensitive, sober
as a mine detector.

Time running out, libido low,
clear the deck
before going below,

stepping thus
into not exactly time
anymore that catches us

snatching a foot
back before it can
take our weight.

83—

Everything dies, though not all at once.
Energy avoids being destroyed
forever, delighting to pounce

changed as it bites
delighted or hard
through our lips.

Pathos of space,
which separates things living
at the same time; pathos

of time, which separates
things living once
and no longer in the same place,

fuse in Piaf's "Je ne regrette
riene," the aching
inescapable power of what accumulates

and recoils in time; with how grace
fades, and what is most loved
is left for last . . .

84—

To have bid
the beginning and the end
lie side by side

in the same bed—(or are they,
like these stacked
stanzas, bridges to nowhere, only

moving forward
because time's text moves
from and toward?)—

does it make them more
all middle
rotating in place, escalator

in mid-air? Or unlike my cats—
angels—at one
with their spirit,

(six black beauties—it's a jungle in here)
if I could afford the chow,
I'd have more.

In their playful, purring way, bless
them, they've somehow
civilized us.

So, no need for recycled owls,
lyrical skylarks,
apparitional seagulls;

nothing worthy of a prize—
(wish granted)—I don't want
to have deserved in the first place.

Then is it worth to delight
in coming crises and convulsion
and have the world prove you right?—

or to have the luck you imagine—
just because you wished it—sure
not to happen?

But isn't it sweet surprise
when the paranoia you've prepped
doesn't materialize?

O, may our luck be like that plane,
ditched and floating, all aboard
safe, on wings in the Hudson.

85—

As perception ignites
roots connecting the field
that enfolds it,

we imagine we could harbor—
despite early and late storms—
each other together.

And where does the new Jerusalem
lead but back to ruin and on
to void? Aerial view over the Judean

desert shows ancient
site digs alongside modern settlements
whose sites in some future present

are excavated, and night brings the glow
of day's resplendent colors
to their end. As one grows

older and things dim, each breath
knows all lords and kings are criminals,
and the King of Crime is Death.

86—

I am trying to pull myself
together to say more than
I know and have to speak of.

Language, please speak—
my tongue assails me
with my mistakes.

Though I have gone
up the ladder of excess no farther
than step one,

broke, dumb, desperate, how badly
I have behaved, skimping the truth
for which I am paying madly.

I have to seize the words passing me
without my vocabulary
of vanity glaring at me continually,

or would the bite
of words I spoke, or didn't,
blow back in spite?

I hear you say terrible, true
words whitened by what's beyond
me, which sometimes do

find me, and I have taken their weight
on the road that springs with
what I would not have seen had I stayed,

though not exactly like a man in need
who goes out, stumbles, looks down, and finds
what he needs at his feet.

A tip, a hint, give us
a leg up in any language you choose,
even ones we don't use

anymore. The world's distances can't quell
nor hide the pleading bursts no longer words
but dread and curses made plosive, distilled

in cell phone Arabic you can hear call
in full-throated cry over the shelling of Aleppo
of the unbelieving and the faithful.

For them, unendurable disaster;
for us, live reality
theater.

Say what you have to say
to more than me; I stand
in my own way.

Won't you translate for
me something new, old,
affording pleasure,

wakening goodbye
to good morning worthy
of new dawn's body?

Must I spell
it out for you who, combined,
contain all spells?

If it's too much to bless,
then make it
language-less.

Though the young dream, plan, connive
wantonly on their way
as their bodies thrive,

living after being born
is not as nimble as a finger
brushing off a thorn.

We live in, on,
through, traces of flow
before song sung, tongue stone . . .

or strewn, then sown. I don't know,
song, stone, strewn, dumb—
I gotta go.

COLOPHON

Spiral Trace was designed at Coffee House Press,
in the historic Grain Belt Brewery's Bottling House
near downtown Minneapolis.
Fonts include Garamond and Celestia Antiqua.

COFFEE HOUSE PRESS

Mission

The mission of Coffee House Press is to publish exciting, vital, and enduring authors of our time; to delight and inspire readers; to contribute to the cultural life of our community; and to enrich our literary heritage. By building on the best traditions of publishing and the book arts, we produce books that celebrate imagination, innovation in the craft of writing, and the many authentic voices of the American experience.

Vision

LITERATURE. We will promote literature as a vital art form, helping to redefine its role in contemporary life. We will publish authors whose groundbreaking work helps shape the direction of 21st-century literature. **WRITERS.** We will foster the careers of our writers by making long-term commitments to their work, allowing them to take risks in form and content. **READERS.** Readers of books we publish will experience new perspectives and an expanding intellectual landscape. **PUBLISHING.** We will be leaders in developing a sustainable 21st-century model of independent literary publishing, pushing the boundaries of content, form, editing, audience development, and book technologies.

Values

Innovation and excellence in all activities
Diversity of people, ideas, and products
Advancing literary knowledge
Community through embracing many cultures
Ethical and highly professional management and governance practices

Good books are brewing at coffeehousepress.org

FUNDER ACKNOWLEDGMENT

Coffee House Press is an independent, nonprofit literary publisher. Our books are made possible through the generous support of grants and gifts from many foundations, corporate giving programs, state and federal support, and through donations from individuals who believe in the transformational power of literature. Coffee House Press receives major operating support from Amazon, the Bush Foundation, the Jerome Foundation, the McKnight Foundation, from Target, and in part from a grant provided by the Minnesota State Arts Board through an appropriation by the Minnesota State Legislature from the State's general fund and its arts and cultural heritage fund with money from the vote of the people of Minnesota on November 4, 2008, and a grant from the Wells Fargo Foundation of Minnesota. Support for this title was received from the National Endowment for the Arts, a federal agency. Coffee House also receives support from: several anonymous donors; Suzanne Allen; Elmer L. and Eleanor J. Andersen Foundation; Around Town Agency; Patricia Beithon; Bill Berkson; the E. Thomas Binger and Rebecca Rand Fund of the Minneapolis Foundation; the Patrick and Aimee Butler Family Foundation; Ruth Dayton; Dorsey & Whitney, LLP; Mary Ebert and Paul Stembler; Chris Fischbach and Katie Dublinski; Fredrikson & Byron, P.A.; Sally French; Anselm Hollo and Jane Dalrymple-Hollo; Jeffrey Hom; Carl and Heidi Horsch; Kenneth Kahn; Alex and Ada Katz; Stephen and Isabel Keating; the Kenneth Koch Literary Estate; Kathy and Dean Koutsky; the Lenfestey Family Foundation; Carol and Aaron Mack; Mary McDermid; Sjur Midness and Briar Andresen; the Nash Foundation; the National Poetry Series; the Rehael Fund of the Minneapolis Foundation; Schwegman, Lundberg & Woessner, P.A.; Kiki Smith; Jeffrey Sugerman and Sarah Schultz; Patricia Tilton; the Archie D. & Bertha H. Walker Foundation; Stu Wilson and Mel Barker; the Woessner Freeman Family Foundation; Margaret and Angus Wurtele; and many other generous individual donors.

ART WORKS.
arts.gov

MINNESOTA
STATE ARTS BOARD

TARGET.

amazon.com

To you and our many readers across the country,
we send our thanks for your continuing support.

Jack Marshall recommends
these Coffee House Press Books

Green Lake Is Awake by Joseph Ceravolo

"This valuable contribution to American poetics restores Ceravolo's boldly asyntactic yet stunningly precise work to book form. . . . His work, blending the sound-sculpting of a Clark Coolidge with deceptively calm, Ashbery-like meditations, carries within it an original and bewitching prosody as delicate as anything in Hopkins."—*Publishers Weekly*

So Recently Rent a World by Andrei Codrescu

A landmark poetry selection that follows the upswell, downfall, and wake of forty-one years of wrestling the muse, *So Recently Rent a World* traverses subjects from aging to consumerism and religion to mass media. Brilliantly funny yet deeply insightful, these poems illuminate Codrescu's acerbic tone and outsized personality and capture the best of his oeuvre.

Portrait and Dream by Bill Berkson

Titled after a Jackson Pollock painting at once figural and abstract, this collection spans nearly fifty years of Bill Berkson's poetry in all its deftness and variety. His poems, full of nuance, intensity, and exuberant wit, spread meaning across the page like quicksilver, creating a body of work suffused with light.

How Long by Ron Padgett

"Padgett's sense of romantic joy is undiminished, as is his thoughtfulness about language and the ways in which time changes meaning, and sense can morph into eloquent absurdity."—*Entertainment Weekly*
2012 PULITZER PRIZE IN POETRY (FINALIST)